First World War
and Army of Occupation
War Diary
France, Belgium and Germany

25 DIVISION
Divisional Troops
Divisional Trench Mortar Batteries
1 March 1917 - 30 April 1918

WO95/2234/3

The Naval & Military Press Ltd
www.nmarchive.com
Published in association with The National Archives

Published by

The Naval & Military Press Ltd

Unit 10 Ridgewood Industrial Park,

Uckfield, East Sussex,

TN22 5QE England

Tel: +44 (0) 1825 749494

www.naval-military-press.com

www.nmarchive.com

This diary has been reprinted in facsimile from the original. Any imperfections are inevitably reproduced and the quality may fall short of modern type and cartographic standards.

© **Crown Copyright**
Images reproduced by permission of The National Archives, London, England, 2015.

Contents

Document type	Place/Title	Date From	Date To
Heading	WO95/2234 13 Divisional Trench Marras Battery		
Heading	Trench Mortar Group Mar 1917-Apr 1918		
War Diary		01/03/1917	31/05/1917
War Diary	Sheet 28 N 36c.	01/06/1917	09/06/1917
War Diary	Letouquet Houplines	10/06/1917	30/06/1917
War Diary	Messages Sector	01/07/1917	05/07/1917
War Diary	G 15c.	09/07/1917	29/07/1917
War Diary	H13c79	30/07/1917	31/07/1917
War Diary	(H.13c6.8) Vlamertinghe	01/08/1917	21/08/1917
War Diary	Steenvoorde	23/08/1917	23/08/1917
War Diary	Vlamertinghe	30/08/1917	05/09/1917
War Diary	Godeswaersvelde	12/09/1917	12/09/1917
War Diary	Steen Becque	16/09/1917	16/09/1917
War Diary	Ames	17/09/1917	26/09/1917
War Diary	Bully Grenay	30/09/1917	07/10/1917
War Diary	Annequin	08/10/1917	01/12/1917
War Diary	Vendin-Lez Bethune	03/12/1917	04/12/1917
War Diary	Boiry Becquerelle	05/12/1917	06/12/1917
War Diary	Boisleux	07/12/1917	07/12/1917
War Diary	St Marc	08/12/1917	08/12/1917
War Diary	Fremicourt	09/12/1917	15/12/1917
War Diary	Baunatre	16/12/1917	31/12/1917
War Diary	Morchies	01/01/1918	14/02/1918
War Diary	Dernancourt	15/02/1918	09/03/1918
War Diary	Camp In L4d.	10/03/1918	31/03/1918
Heading	D. T. M. O. 25th Division. April 1918		
War Diary	Ploegsteert Area	01/04/1918	25/04/1918
War Diary	Meterew Sector	26/04/1918	30/04/1918

WO/95/2234

/3 Divisional Trench Mortars
Battery

25TH DIVISION
DIVL ARTILLERY

TRENCH MORTAR GROUP
MAR 1917 - APR 1918

25TH DIVISION
DIVL ARTILLERY

For the month of MARCH 1917. March page 1

Army Form C. 2118

WAR DIARY of DTMO's Group.
INTELLIGENCE SUMMARY 25th Division
(Erase heading not required.)

Vol 9

Place	Date	Hour	Summary of Events and Information	Remarks and references to Appendices
	1		In action on divisional front from R LYS northward to ANTON'S FARM, north west of St YVES. No operations of importance. Attached to N.Z. Division	Partm
	2		D°	Partm
	3		Officers of TMB attended one day course at TM school at BERTHEN. Difficulty of transport overcome by kindness of #2 3rd Bde NZFA who lent horses	Partm
	4		Nothing of importance	Partm
	5		d°	Partm
	6			Partm
	7			Partm
	8		NZ Trench Mortars arrived and began taking over	Partm
	9		Taking over completed	Partm
	10		Rest and cleaning up	Partm
	11		Batteries moved up to LUMBRES by rail to ST OMER but should have gone in lorries when failed to arrive. DTMO remained for rail haison into NZ DTMO	Partm
	12		Lorries arrived in the evening & moved kits & stores to LUMBRES. 4 lorries just enough	Partm
	13		Battery training at LUMBRES begun	Partm
	14		Training at LUMBRES	Partm
	15		" "	Partm
	16		" "	Partm
	17		DTMO from NZ division to LUMBRES	Partm
	18		Training	Partm
	19		Trench Mortar competition at horse shoes, turn out and drill one mortar per battery judged by Major Duke DSO Bde Major & Captain Somerville SMK (late DTMO) RFA. Result 2/25 1. X/25 2. Y/25 3.	Partm
	20		Training	Partm
	21		March to BEARING HEM. Only two lorries provided, two journeys had to be made 2 head arrived 11 pm	Partm
	22		Marched to RUE VERTE VIEUX BERQUIN. 5 lorries for transport very satisfactory	Partm
	23		Training resumed	Partm

Phillimore
DTMO -

March page 2

1917 Army Form C. 2118

WAR DIARY
or
INTELLIGENCE SUMMARY
(Erase heading not required.)

Instructions regarding War Diaries and Intelligence Summaries are contained in F.S. Regs., Part II. and the Staff Manual respectively. Title Pages will be prepared in manuscript.

Place	Date	Hour	Summary of Events and Information	Remarks and references to Appendices
	24		Training at RUE VERTE	Parvon Parvern
	25		do	Parvern
	26		do	Par Vern
	27		do	Par Ven
	28		Marched to NEUF BERQUIN transport four GS wagons, doing a double journey. Train was satisfactory	Par Ven
	29		Training resumed	Par Ven Parvern
	30		Training	Par Ven
	31		Party of Officers sent up to the line to reconnoitre new position	Parvern

PM Wentworth Hunter
Captain OTM⁰
25th Do

WAR DIARY or INTELLIGENCE SUMMARY

Army Form C. 2118

Month of April 1917

Dual TMs
25th Div

Place	Date	Hour	Summary of Events and Information	Remarks and references to Appendices
	April 1			
	2		Ballieux en rest at NEUF BERQUIN	
	3		Working party 110 all ranks proceeded to NEUVE EGLISE to dig positions for medium TMB.	
	4		Work commenced on TMB emplacements	
	5			
	6			
	7		TMB details joined main party at NEUVE EGLISE. NZ medium TMs relieved in WULVERGHEM sector.	
	8		In relief NEUVE EGLISE. Work on positions for medium TMs carried on.	
	9			
	10			
	11			
	12			
	13			
	14		Positions for heavy TMs reconnoitred	
	15		Work on heavy TM positions begun; medium continued	
	16			
	17			
	18			
	19			
	20			
	21			
	22			
	23			
	24	4 p	13 rds fired on German wire from medium TMs. 6 rounds 30 mortars most successful no casualties	
	25	5 p	13 rds fired - do - do - 2 wounded by own	
	26		shrapnel. 8 p one slight one dangerous. Three two shots pierced the machine cabs of NEWTDM aim-em beds for 2" TMs.	
	27		1 OR killed, 1 wounded by hostile A.2. shell. work continued	
	28	5.15 p	37 rds fired on German wire from 9 mortars. 15 minute repetition 30 minutes shoot most successful	
			2 OR killed, 1 wounded by 2" punctures.	
	29		Work on emplacements carried on	
	30		Handed over 4 NZ dugouts leaving X/25 TMB safely under orders of DTMO NZ divn	

May 1917

Army Form C. 2118.

2 T.M. Bty's

WAR DIARY
or
INTELLIGENCE SUMMARY.
(Erase heading not required.)

Instructions regarding War Diaries and Intelligence
Summaries are contained in F. S. Regs., Part II
and the Staff Manual respectively. Title pages
will be prepared in manuscript.

Place	Date	Hour	Summary of Events and Information	Remarks and references to Appendices
	1.5.17		Went into rest billets at NEUF BERQUIN. X Bty remained in line under N.Z. Divn	
	10.5.17		Returned into WULVERGHEM SECTOR. Z Bty relieved X. in the line	
	11.5.17		Old positions re-manned. Work recommenced on medium Bty emplacements.	
	12.5.17 13.5.17 16.5.17		Report by O.T.M.O. on positions for new scheme approved by CRA. 3 Importation chairs in Michelin shop in Nieppe Quarters betwn [?] to stop netting given. 196 rounds fired Medium Batteries front no trouble to C.O.L. I am sorry there was to even a raid	
	19.5.17		Medium Batteries fired 4/12th. two prematures 3 casualties	
	24.5.17		T.M. fired in support of 74th Inf Bde Raid.	
	27&28/5/17		All T.M. orders into line in readiness. 2 mortars per battery were to have been in Coy.	
	29.5.17 30.5.17 31.5.17		Heavy shooting completed and guns mounted X Bty Giddis shelled 2 Kancettes Nieppe shoot Organised daily shooting on enemy supports subject as any given Commander a raider able suitably, owing to enemy shelling	

Ouch J Cunningham
Capt R.a. Bg Two

JUNE 1917

T.M. Burry
25 Division

Army Form C. 2118.

WAR DIARY
or
INTELLIGENCE SUMMARY.
(Erase heading not required.)

Instructions regarding War Diaries and Intelligence Summaries are contained in F. S. Regs., Part II. and the Staff Manual respectively. Title pages will be prepared in manuscript.

Place	Date	Hour	Summary of Events and Information	Remarks and references to Appendices
Sheet 28 N.36.c.	1.6.17		Medium Batteries shelled NUTMEG RESERVE with 610 rounds, hns positions in front line west. The Heavies opened on BELL FARM & ONTARIO. 60 rounds.	
"	2.6.17		Mediums shelled NUTMEG: 1254 rounds. Heavies fired 90 on enemy batteries. Many good hits on UGLY RESERVE, Gnd 1,250 Kms up our Battn H.Q.	
	3.6.17		Mediums fired 1004 on NUTMEG RESERVE. Aeroplane photo of 4.6.17 showed NUTMEG RESERVE obliterated almost entirely. Heavies fired 103 rounds.	
	4.6.17. 5.6.17		Mediums fired on enemy front-line 972 rounds Heavies fired 83 rounds. The Batteries water tank Withyls ham hrs retaliated very little. Enemy at 9.15pm. he las blasted intense bombardment of front line area.	
	6.6.17	12pm	At Noon we fired 807 rounds medium 70 rounds heavy. Med on Enmy support lines NUTMEG & UGLY; HEAVIES on UGLY RESERVE, BELL FARM & DUGOUTS between GRAY ONTARIO FARM. Bhs thereof withdrawn	
	7.6.17	3.10am	MESSINES RIDGE ATTACKED & TAKEN.	
	9.6.17		Received orders to pass under the command CRA III Aust Div.	
LE TOUQUET – HOUPLINES	10.6.17		Medium & heavy positions reconnoitred in LE TOUQUET – HOUPLINES sector. Gunner Aston killed near GASOMETER CORNER.	
	14.6.17		6 L'ng Russian Tms taken up line : 3 taken into HOUPLINES, 3 to motor car corner. Working parties were heavily shelled both in line & in billets. H.Q. moved to B2'c (Sht 36)	

JUNE 1917
Army Form C. 2118.

WAR DIARY
or
INTELLIGENCE SUMMARY.
(Erase heading not required.)

T.M. Batt.
25th Division

Place	Date	Hour	Summary of Events and Information	Remarks and references to Appendices
LE TOUQUET — HOUPLINES	15.6.17	1.30 pm	LT KILPIN & 3 other ranks (16th Divⁿ attached) wounded at BURNT OUT FARM. LT KILPIN died of wounds in about one hour. Buried at Dressing Station Cemetery at PONT D'ACHELLES. LT ARKWRIGHT & 8 other ranks more or less seriously wounded in streets of Armentières. N.C.O. & Champ & Trumpet wounded at HQrs	
	17.6.17		Moved back to old billets in field at T8c (sheet 28)	
	25.6.17		Resting & cleaning stores &c	
	27.6.17 to 30.6.17		Salved ammunition around our old positions in N36a & T6 &c. Loading parties for D.A.C. moving back ammunition from old front areas.	

Bnn J. Cunningham
Lt R.a.
for D.T.M.O.
30/6/17

25th Div. T.M. Bde.

WAR DIARY or INTELLIGENCE SUMMARY

JULY 1917 Army Form C. 2118.

Place	Date	Hour	Summary of Events and Information	Remarks and references to Appendices
MESSINES SECTOR G.15.c.	1-3		During this time the Bde. furnished fatigue parties to assist 26th D.A.C. in obtaining ammunition in the MESSINES SECTOR.	
	5th		The Bde. moved from camp near NEUVE EGLISE to GISC (near POPERINGHE)	
	9th		The Bde., having come under the control of the 8th D.A., began the transport of ammunition nightly from MENIN ROAD DUMP to 6" and 2" RAILWAY COPSE where work on 4 x 2" emplacements was also begun.	
	13th		Lt. AITCHISON fired 30 rounds registration. From this time on till 27th, the Bde. was held by medium batteries (1 + 2) for eight-day periods, X Battery being called upon to reinforce Z Battery. All NCOs and men otherwise available were employed nightly on bomb carrying. Officers times in the line lived in the dugouts at RAILWAY COPSE, whilst the working parties were taken nightly by motor lorries to a point on near MENIN ROAD DRESSING STATION as possible.	
	14th		350 rounds fired (2" T.M.) on front line system in I.12.c. (SHARP 'N'O)	
	15th		100 " " " " " " " " " "	
	16th		60 " " " " " " " " " "	
	17th		120 " " " " " " " " " "	

2/28th. Div. T.M. Bde.

Army Form C. 2118.

JULY 1917 (cont.)

WAR DIARY
or
INTELLIGENCE SUMMARY.
(Erase heading not required.)

Instructions regarding War Diaries and Intelligence Summaries are contained in F. S. Regs., Part II. and the Staff Manual respectively. Title pages will be prepared in manuscript.

Place	Date	Hour	Summary of Events and Information	Remarks and references to Appendices
G 15 c.	18th		The Bde sustained severe military personal loss in the deaths of CAPT. P.M. CHAWORTH-MUSTERS, R.I.C. R.F.A. (I.T.M.O.) and LT. A. DAVOREN R.G.A. (O.C. 2/25) who with the D.T.M.O. 8th Div. were killed by a shell 2 Lt W.T. VOSS, R.F.A. (X/125) was seriously wounded in the face by the same shell. 50 rounds fired by LT. DAVOREN on I.12.c.1. (2" M).	
	19th		50 " " " " " " " " enemy strong pts " " " " LT. MITCHISON " " [1] LLoyd 2 m/c emplacements " " " " " " " killed 2 men, 3 Wynded.	
	20th		CAPT. L.W. CALDWELL, M.C., R.F.H. appointed D.T.M.O.	
	21st		2" T.Ms fired 100 rounds on I.12 a. One 2" T.M. in action. One destroyed by replacement (6 dumps)	
	22nd		2" TMs fired 100 " " " " at MENIN ROAD.	
			W/Stokes TMB. began work on emplacement at —	
	23-9		at different times of the day, the 2" TMs under Gun officer's 8 D.A.T.Ms fired about 150 rds. 2 Mortars	Casualties
	28-9		" " " " " " fired about 50 rounds	
			" " " " " At 24-15	
			During this time attempts to arrange for infantry working parties failed save on one occasion. The T.M. Bde provided, by means of its own personnel, its own supply of ammunition. Casualties sustained numbered 32 :- of these 14 were due to gas (all returned to unit); 5 were killed (2 officers + 3 gunners) : 10 were wounded + evacuated (1 officer + S.N.C.O. 4 gunners): 1 wounded gunner returned to his unit. 21 of the total casualties were sustained by carrying parties — including gas casualties. A.H.	

Army Form C. 2118.

25th Div. T.M. Bde.

Instructions regarding War Diaries and Intelligence Summaries are contained in F.S. Regs., Part II. and the Staff Manual respectively. Title pages will be prepared in manuscript.

WAR DIARY
or
INTELLIGENCE SUMMARY.
(Erase heading not required.)

JULY 1917 (Contd) (3)

Place	Date	Hour	Summary of Events and Information	Remarks and references to Appendices
G.15.c.	25.		Heavies fired 6 rounds for registration on targets in T.12.a & b.	
	26		" " 17 " " " " T.12.a + g.	
	29		" " 22 rounds on T.12.a.b.	
			On the morning of this day, the personnel of T.M. Bde. was withdrawn from the line.	
H.13.c.7.9	30		T.M. Bde moved camp to H.13.c.7.9.	
	31.	3.50am	ZERO.	

Lieut J. Cunningham
RFA
for D.T.M.O.

1.8.17.

25th Div. T.M. Group. August 1917.
25-D TM Bys
SH 14

WAR DIARY or INTELLIGENCE SUMMARY
Army Form C. 2118.
(Erase heading not required.)

Place	Date	Hour	Summary of Events and Information	Remarks and references to Appendices
(H.13c.6.8) VLAMERTINGHE	1.8.17		T.M. Brigade in rest billets. Weather exceedingly wet. Positions in line waterlogged.	
WINNIPEG	2.8.17 –6.8.17		2 Detachments of 2 N.C.O. + 10 men employed H.Q.R.E. at WINNIPEG DUMP daily.	
"	7.8.17 –10.8.17		Detachments of 1 ON.C.O + 30 men employed daily H/QRE at WINNIPEG, ACTON St KRUISTRAAT.	
	10.8.17		LTS AITCHISON & WILLIAMS reconnoitred old front line positions & salved guns & material. Then were brought down to billets the following night along with 2" T.M. heads from LILLE GATE.	
	19.8.17		4 Parties of 1 NCO + 3 men sent into the line at MOATED FARM to form guard for the guns of 110th B.K.R.A.	
	21.8.17		T.M. 13cc began work on taking up ammunition to from damaged battery positions on both sides of railway in I.15c. (Sheet 28).	
STEENVOORDE	23.8.17		T.M. Group came to STEENVOORDE to rest billets.	
VLAMERTINGHE	30.9.17		Returned to old camping ground near VLAMERTINGHE. (H.13c.6.8)	

J. Caldwell Capt
D.A.T.M.O
25th Division

SEPTEMBER 1917

25 Dn T.M. Group

WAR DIARY
INTELLIGENCE SUMMARY

Place	Date	Hour	Summary of Events and Information	Remarks and references to Appendices
LOOS SECTOR	1.9.17		Fatigue parties supplied to R.E. for work in YPRES. These parties were found daily till 9.9.17.	
"	5.9.17		Took over the T.M. material of II Corps.	
GODESWAERSVELDE	12.9.17		T.M. Group moved into Ant Fields of this village	
STEENBEEQUE	16.9.17		T.M. " moved into LIÉTAL "TROUPES" (THIENNES)	
AMES	17.9.17		T.M. moved into AMES area till 1st Filled Terrace till 29.9.17	
"	24.9.17		R.G. Sports at AMETTES	
"	26.9.17		Divisional 6th at AUCHOURIZ.	
BULLY-GRENAY	30.9.17		T.M. Group marched into BULLY GRENAY	
	1.10.17			

Army Form C. 2118.

WAR DIARY
or
INTELLIGENCE SUMMARY.
(Erase heading not required.)

25th TRENCH MORTAR GROUP.

October 1917. Page 1.

Place	Date	Hour	Summary of Events and Information	Remarks and references to Appendices
BULLY-GRENAY.	1st.		D.T.M.O. and Battery Commanders reconnoitred for 6" Newton positions in front of LENS.	
	2nd.		do. do.	
	3rd.		do. do.	
	4th.		All Batteries sent forward working parties to dig 6" Newton and 9.45" emplacements.	
	5th.		Working parties billeted at CITE du MOULIN.	
	6th.		All Batteries working on emplacements.	
	7th.		Working parties returned to BULLY-GRENAY.	
ANNEQUIN.	8th.		The T.M.Group moved to ANNEQUIN in XI Corps area. The 25th Div.T.M.Group relieved the 2nd Div. T.M.Group in the CAMBRIN, CANAL, and GIVENCHY Sectors	
	9th.		Y. Battery in the North, X Battery in the centre, and Z. Battery in the South.	
	10th.		The 6th PORTUGUESE Medium T.M. Battery attached to the 25th Div. T.M. Group. Lt. G.D.WILLIAMS, M.C. returned from Hospital and took command of Y/45 Medium Battery. 2nd Lieut. J.D.GRAY and 2nd Lieut. R.S.GILLESPIE joined Z/25 M.T.M. Battery.	
	11th.		All Batteries building new positions in their own sectors. 3 Platoons of the SOUTH WALES BORDERERS (pioneers) lent to the T.M. Group to help work on positions.	
	12th.		do.	
	13th.		All Batteries building positions.	

Army Form C. 2118.

WAR DIARY
or
INTELLIGENCE SUMMARY.
(Erase heading not required)

25th TRENCH MORTAR GROUP.

October. 1917. Page 2.

Place	Date	Hour	Summary of Events and Information	Remarks and references to Appendices
ANNEQUIN.	14th.		All Batteries building positions.	
	15th.		2nd Lieut. D.J. ROACH posted from 25th D.A.C. to W/25 Heavy T.M.B.	
	16th.		All Batteries building new positions. 2nd Lieut. GORDON transferred from Z/25 to the R.F.C.	
	17th.		All Batteries building new positions.	
	18th.		All Batteries working on new positions. 2nd Lieut. GRAY went to 1st Army T.M.School.	
	19th.		All Batteries working on new positions.	
	20th.		do.	
	21st.		do.	
	22nd.		do.	
	23rd.		One man of Z/25 wounded.	
	24th.		One man of W/25 wounded.	
	25th.	11.5am. to 12.5pm	A Bombardment with wire cutting was carried out by 12 2" Morters between A.22.s24-A.21.d.93 and A.27.b.9535 and A.28.c.18. 356 rounds were fired in all. Wire was reported cut, and trench much damaged. One N.C.O. of X Battery wounded.	
	26th.		-------	
	27th.		-------	

25th TRENCH MORTAR GROUP

October 1917.

WAR DIARY
or
INTELLIGENCE SUMMARY.
(Erase heading not required.)

* Instructions regarding War Diaries and Intelligence Summaries are contained in F. S. Regs., Part II. and the Staff Manual respectively. Title pages will be prepared in manuscript.

Place	Date	Hour	Summary of Events and Information
ANNEQUIN.	28th.		2nd Lieut. GRAY returned from 1st Army Trench Mortar School.
	29th.		-------
	30th.		-------
	31st.		-------
			1248 rounds 2" fired during October.
			156 " 9.45" " "
			Casualties:- 2 N.C.O's and 4 men.

*Army Form C. 2118.

WAR DIARY
or
INTELLIGENCE SUMMARY.
(Erase heading not required.)

Instructions regarding War Diaries and Intelligence Summaries are contained in F.S. Regs., Part II and the Staff Manual respectively. Title pages will be prepared in manuscript.

25th French Mortar Bry.
November 1917 Page 1

Vol 17

Place	Date	Hour	Summary of Events and Information	Remarks and references to Appendices
ANNEQUIN	1		Batteries making new emplacements and preparing for one	
	2	10 AM	A Bombardment with wirecutting was carried out by 12 2 in and 6 H.S mork	
		6	(Between A10.15.20 and A9.6.95.50) 440 rounds 2in and 15 rounds 6 inch were fired	
	3	9.15AM	A Bombardment with wirecutting was carried out by 12 2 in and 3 6" in in enemy trenches	
			between A10 15.20 and A9 6 95.50 400 rounds 2in 6 was 6" rounds 6" in were fired	
	4	10.30	A Bombardment with wire cutting was carried out by 12 2in and 3 6.5 in in the enemy trenches	
		6	between A10 15.23 and A9 6.95.50 488 2 rounds 2in and 15 rounds 6.5 in were fired Enemy made no	
		11.30AM	Trenches were ripped old much damaged	
	5		A quiet day	
	6		A quiet day	
	7		A Bombardment with wirecutting was carried out by 8 2in T.M and 4 T.Ms in the between & SC 15.05 and	
			234.00 o 552 rounds 2in and 95 rounds 6 in were fired. Wire was cut and trenches much damaged	
	8			
	9		Batteries moving up positions after first shoot	
	10		Batteries fired 4 two rounds no retaliation	
	11			
	12			

T2134. Wt. W708—776. 500000. 4/15. Sir J. C. & S.

Army Form C. 2118.

WAR DIARY
or
INTELLIGENCE SUMMARY.
(Erase heading not required.)

Page 2

Place	Date	Hour	Summary of Events and Information	Remarks and references to Appendices
ANNEQUIN	13		C.R.A. 4th Div: fired in retaliation for hostile Trench Mortar fire	
	14		- - - -	
	15		2/3/1st Wilts: joined T.M. Group and were partial to X Bty	
	16		C.A. 4 did not fire as retaliation as hostile Trench Mortars	
	17		- - -	
	18		- - -	
	19		Lieut. D. Wade rejoined 2/23 T.M. Bty from hospital	
	20	3 pm	A Great demonstration of the Enemys was followed A/OG.143 and A/96.75 was carried out by 8 am.	
		4 pm	T.M. fired 3 GAS in T.M. 363 rounds 2 in. and 48 rounds 9.45 in. were fired in all. The affair appeared to	
	21		be very quiet.	
			- - -	
	22		2/Lieut E. STEARNE's joined the T.M. group and is posted to 1/23 T.M. Bty. Lieut. A.T. CUNNINGHAM posted to B	
			Company of 2/23 S T.M. Bty. 2/Lieut WM UPTON posted to Hd Qrs T.M. group vice Lieut CUNNINGHAM.	
	23		- - - -	
	24	2 pm	Bombardment on TOWPATH ALLEY and A/OC.25'S' and Age 57.42 1/25 T.M.B. 787 Gunners 2 in. W/25 T.M.5 25/Md.	
		3 pm		

T2134. Wt. W708—776. 500000. 4/15. Sir J. C. & S.

WAR DIARY
or
INTELLIGENCE SUMMARY.

Army Form C. 2118.

(Erase heading not required.)

Hour	Summary of Events and Information	Remarks and references to Appendices

...y trenches by 2/25 T.M.B. and W/25 T.M.B. on A.29.c.20.75 and N.28.a.90.05

3774 rounds 2" fired during November
446   "   "   "   "   "
130   6"   "   "   "   "

Casualties - 4 N.C.O.s and 8 men

A. Michael Capt
D.T.M.O.
25th Divn.

2/12/17

Army Form C. 2118.

WAR DIARY
INTELLIGENCE SUMMARY.
(Erase heading not required.)

25th Divl T.M. Group DECEMBER 1917

Instructions regarding War Diaries and Intelligence Summaries are contained in F. S. Regs., Part II. and the Staff Manual respectively. Title pages will be prepared in manuscript.

Place	Date	Hour	Summary of Events and Information	Remarks and references to Appendices
ANNEQUIN	1/12/17		25th Divl T.M. Group was relieved by the 42nd Divl T.M's in CANAL & KINGSWAY Sector and by the 46th Divl T.M's in the CAMBRIN Sector. 25th Divl T.M. Group moved into Training Area Tel Enfer – ENQUIN-LEZ-BETHUNE.	
VENDIN-LEZ-BETHUNE	3/12/17		Parties working under entraining officer BETHUNE STATION, to entrain 25th DIVISIONAL ARTILLERY	
			Lieut A Dewar Z/25 TM Bg transferred to 110th Bde R.F.A.	
	4/12/17		As on 3rd inst	
BOIRY-BECQUERELLE	5/12/17		Entrained at BETHUNE for 3rd Army Area (5th Corps) Detrained at BOISLEUX-au-MONT and moved into hutments on the HENIN Road near BOIRY-BECQUERELLE. Lieut W.E. Green joined W/25 TM Bg	
	6/12/17		Cleaning up camp and awaiting further instructions	
BOISLEUX ST MARC	7/12/17		Moved into hutments at BOISLEUX ST MARC	
	8/12/17		Cleaning up camps, guns stores etc and awaiting further orders	
FREMICOURT	9/12/17		Moved into VI Corps Area at FREMICOURT on the BAPAUME – CAMBRAI Road.	
	10/12/17		D.T.M.O. and officers reconnoitring positions about to takeover over from 36th Divisional Trench Mortars in front of QUEANT	

BRONVILLE

Sheet 2.

Army Form C. 2118.

WAR DIARY
or
INTELLIGENCE SUMMARY.
(Erase heading not required.)

Instructions regarding War Diaries and Intelligence Summaries are contained in F. S. Regs., Part II. and the Staff Manual respectively. Title pages will be prepared in manuscript.

Place	Date	Hour	Summary of Events and Information	Remarks and references to Appendices
FREMICOURT	11/3/17		25th Divisional T.M. Groups which & 56th Divl T.M.s - V/25 T.M.Bdy relieve V/56 T.M.Bdy. but V/25 T.M.Bdy & Z/25 T.M.Bdy relieve the Medium T.M. Battery 56th Division. V/25, Y/25 and Z/25 T.M.Bs move into billets on the VAUX – NEUVILLES Road. H.Q T.M Group and X/25 T.M.Bdy remained at FREMICOURT	
	12/3/17		Registration carried out by X/25, Y/25 and Z/25 T.M. Bdys	
	13/3/17		No special action. Enemy retaliates	
	14/3/17		do	
	15/3/17		do	
	17/3/17		Batteries working on positions	
BARASTRE	18/3/17		Batteries working on positions. S.O. 25th T.M. Group moved into huts on 293 Army Heavy Artillery Brigade in the BAPAUME – VAULX Road about mid way between BAPAUME and BARASTRE. X/25 T.M.Bdy moved into billets with Y, Z /25 T.M. Bdys also. MIRAMIES. Lieut. ECESTERNES and 10 other Ranks proceeded to 2nd Army T.M. School, 20 Seville Hatton Scout DJ ROACH & 16 other Ranks returned from 1st Army T.M. School. X/25 T.M.Bdy relieved Y/25 T.M.Bdy on the Line. no special action.	

Army Form C. 2118.

WAR DIARY
or
INTELLIGENCE SUMMARY.
(Erase heading not required.)

Sheet 3

Place	Date	Hour	Summary of Events and Information	Remarks and references to Appendices
SOUASTRE	19/12/17		Batteries working on positions. No special news.	
	20/12/17		do	
	21/12/17		20 M/188 to Scopton and engineers for No. special action. Working on positions	
	22/12/17		do	
	23/12/17		do	
	24/12/17		Y/25 T.M.Bty relieved X/25 T.M.Bty in the line	
	25/12/17		No special action	
	26/12/17		Working on positions. No special action	
	27/12/17		do	
	28/12/17		do	
	29/12/17		Rank/ Warm proceeded on a few days leave at IV Corps School	
	30/12/17		Working on positions. No special action	
	31/12/17		X/25 T.M.Bty relieved Y/25 T.M.Bty on the line 1/25 T.M.Bty fired 6 "7 P.M." T of 36 T.M.Rof Field Ammn 9.25 P.M. in co-operation with Heavy Artillery. 16 Rds	
			Total Casualties = Nil	
			Total Ammunition Fired = { 9.45" = 35 , 6" = 103 }	
			A.Forsch Lieut R.F.A. for D.T.M.O. /25 M Division	

Sheet No. 1.

Army Form C. 2118.

Instructions regarding War Diaries and Intelligence Summaries are contained in F. S. Regs., Part II. and the Staff Manual respectively. Title pages will be prepared in manuscript.

WAR DIARY
or
INTELLIGENCE SUMMARY.
(Erase heading not required.)

January 1918.   25th Bord T.M. Group

Vol 19

Place	Date	Hour	Summary of Events and Information	Remarks and references to Appendices
MORCHIES.	1-1-18		Working on Positions. No T.M. firing.	
"	2-1-18		Medium T.M'S. fired 40 rounds 6" in accordance with orders. Remarks anything re Positions etc. Men detailed from Infantry Groups (Infantry). Working on Positions. No T.M. activity.	
"	3-1-18		"	
"	4-1-18		"	
"	5-1-18		"	
"	6-1-18		" 2nd Lt Wilson 4th D.T.M. Borned in corral at Lagnicourt T.M. School.	
"	7-1-18		Medium T.M.S. fired 6 rounds 3" for registration purposes. Also Positions sending say. 25 Stokes & 10 T/Ps report from 3rd Army T.M. School.	
"	8-1-18		Heavies fired 11 rounds 9.45" and Mediums 21 rds 6" in accordance operation order. (Rferry.) Report reported from Hospital 1/25 reported T/25 also 8 rds 9" x 6" Lost 2 rds 9.45" Lost 2 rds 9" x 6" fired 45 rounds no casualty strong arm formed in accordance and operation orders.	
"	9-1-18		Heavies fired 5 rds 9.45" Mediums fired rounds 6" in accordance ordinary routine work.	
"	10-1-18		Nothing except ordinary routine.	
"	11-1-18		"	
"	12-1-18		10 T/Ps 6" fired on Enry strong point.	
"	13-1-18		Nothing except ordinary routine 1/25 reported off 1/25 in to Line. No T.M. activity	
"	14-1-18		"	
"	15-1-18		Ordinary Routine. No strong action taken	
"	16/1/10			

(A7930). Wt. W12859/M1293. 750,000. 1/17. D. D. & L., Ltd. Forms/C.2118/14.

Army Form C. 2118.

WAR DIARY
or
INTELLIGENCE SUMMARY.
(Erase heading not required.)

Place	Date	Hour	Summary of Events and Information	Remarks and references to Appendices
MORCHIES	17/1/18		Ordinary Routine, working on position etc. No action taken.	
"	18/1/18		"	
"	19/1/18		2/Lt E.C. Stevens R.F.A. to Hospital (sick)	
"	20/1/18		Nothing except ordinary routine work. 22nd Wilshs. & 9/DLI relieved by 3rd A. & S. Hr. & 7th Camerons 62nd Div.	
"	21/1/18		No relief by 1/25 on that date. — No news received as to this relief.	
"	22/1/18		Nothing except ordinary routine.	
"	23/1/18		1 O.R. promoted to the Corps' School, 1 O.R. promoted to 14 Corps Rec School, 1 Off. & 1 O.R. attached from 57 Div. T.M.S.	
"	24/1/18		1 Off & 1 O.R. attached from 57 Div. T.M.B.	
"	25/1/18			
"	26/1/18			
"	27/1/18		Lt. J.P. Morgan-Coke to C/112 Brigade R.F.A. 1 O.R. proceeded on ordinary course at 33rd Div. Lewis Battery R.G.A.	1/25
"	28/1/18		5 O.Rs. proceeded on ordinary course at 33rd Div. Lewis School, attached from 57 Div. T.M.B.	
"	29/1/18		1/25 now relieved by 1/25 in Estrees — Battery Routine, working on position etc.	
"	30/1/18		"	
"	31/1/18		1 O.R. proceeded on coaching to 219 Siege Battery R.G.A.	

TOTAL CASUALTIES. = Nil
TOTAL AMMUNITION FIRED { 9.45" 241 Rounds
                       { 6" 161 Rounds

H. Roach 2/Lt R.F.A
J.S. ?? T.M.O. /25

Army Form C. 2118.

WAR DIARY
or
INTELLIGENCE SUMMARY
(Erase heading not required.)

FEBRUARY 1918. 25th Divl. T.M. GROUP.

Place	Date	Hour	Summary of Events and Information	Remarks and references to Appendices
MORCHIES.	1		Batteries working on positions etc.	
	2		- ditto -	
	3		- ditto -	
	4		Y Battery relieved X Battery in the Line.	
	5		Batteries working on positions etc.	
	6	2 - 2.15 p.m.	A concentrated shoot on the QUEANT BIRDCAGE was carried out by 5 6" and 2 9.45" T.M's as a demonstration. 12 rounds 9.45" and 160 rounds 6" were fired. The xxx shoot was reported satisfactory.	
	7		Medium 6" T.M. fired 3 rounds for registration.	
	8		T.M. activity Nil. Batteries working on positions.	
	9		- ditto -	
	10		- ditto -	
	11		X Battery relieved Y Battery in the Line.	
	12		Medium 6" T.M's fired 8 rounds in registration.	
	13			
	14		6th Division T.M. Group relieved the 25th Divl. T.M. Group on the 25th Divl. Front. 25th T.M. Group went out to DERNANCOURT to train. The 6th and 51st Divisions each had one Officer and 18 O.R's of the 25th T.M. Group, attached to them to man 6 reserve 6" Trench Mortars on their respective fronts. 1 Officer and 20 men were sent to the IV Corps Reinforcement Camp at ACHIET-le-PETIT to work on the PUISIEUX Artillery Range.	
DERNAN-COURT.	15) 16) 17) 18) 19) 20) 21)		Daily Parades, inspections and Drill under Supervision of O's.C. Batteries.	
	22		The Officers and men attached to the 6th and 51st Divisions and the IV Corps Reinforcement Camp were relieved by equal numbers. The personnel relieved returned to DERNANCOURT.	

Sheet 2.

Army Form C. 2118.

WAR DIARY
or
~~INTELLIGENCE~~ SUMMARY
(Erase heading not required.)

25th DIVL. T.M. GROUP.

BEBRUARY 1918.

Place	Date	Hour	Summary of Events and Information	Remarks and references to Appendices
DERNAN-COURT.	23) 24) 25) 26) 27)		Daily Parades, inspections and Drill under supervision of O's.C. Batteries.	
	28		The Officers and men attached to the 6th and 51st Divisions and the IV Corps Reinforcement Camp were relieved by equal numbers. The personnel relieved returned to DERNANCOURT.	
			Total Casualties. .... NIL.	
			Total Ammunition fired) 9.45" 12 rounds.) 6" 174 rounds.	

[signature]
Captain R.F.A.
D.T.M.O., 25th Division.

Army Form C. 2118.

25th T.M. GROUP.

WAR DIARY
or
INTELLIGENCE SUMMARY.
(Erase heading not required.)

MARCH 1918.

Place	Date	Hour	Summary of Events and Information	Remarks and references to Appendices
DERNANCOURT	1.		Batteries training.	
	2.		do	
	3.		do	
	4.		Reorganisation of Batteries took place. Captain Ansell-Wicks M.C. of W/25 H.T.M.B. took over Command of V & VI Corps Heavy T.M.B. W. X, Y & Z Medium Batteries split up into two Medium Btys X & Y Canadians of 53 men each. Lt. G.D. Howel M.C. posted to Command Y/25 T.M.B. with twenty-eight men Williams M.C. posted to X/25 T.M.B with twenty six men. 2nd Lt. Phipps posted to X/25 T.M.B rank of senior to Colonel acquired to make up X & Y Btys were taken from W/25 H.T.M.B. remainder of W/25 went to V/IV Corps H.T.M.B. Officers & gun teams organized after reorganisation.	
	5.		Transferred to 4th Brigade R.F.A. Bank	
	6.		Batteries training	
	7.		do	
	8.		Permanently attached to the 5th & 51st Divisions in the line who relieved by equal number of men from DERNANCOURT. BRUNEHAMEL relieved by fifty the to DERNANCOURT.	
	9.		25th T.M. Grp. Moved from DERNANCOURT to camp on the ACHIET-LE-PETIT	
CAMP in L.4.d.	10.		- BUCQUOY road in L.4.d. - Batteries training.	

Army Form C. 2118.

25th Div: Artillery ?
March 1918

WAR DIARY
or
INTELLIGENCE SUMMARY.
(Erase heading not required.)

Place	Date	Hour	Summary of Events and Information	Remarks and references to Appendices
Q M P ink	11.		Batteries training	
L.A.D.	12.		C.R.A. inspected the Trench Mortar Group.	
	13.		G.O.C. 25th Division inspected the Trench Mortar Group.	
	14.		Personnel attached to the 15th & 51st Divisions in the line returned.	
			An equal number of men Personnel returned to Corps sheets L+d. Batteries training.	
	15.		do	
	16.		do	
	17.		do	
	18.		do	
	19.		do	
	20.		Batys moved to n: army attack start	Acting as escort to Div: Arty H.Q.
	21.		With enemy orders to Petit	
	22.		moved to Achut to Petit	
	23.		Movement of	
	24.		moved to Glencamp	
	25.		" — Somain	
	26.		" — Luchuilen	
	27.			

Army Form C. 2118.

WAR DIARY
or
INTELLIGENCE SUMMARY.
(Erase heading not required.)

Instructions regarding War Diaries and Intelligence Summaries are contained in F. S. Regs., Part II. and the Staff Manual respectively. Title pages will be prepared in manuscript.

Place	Date	Hour	Summary of Events and Information	Remarks and references to Appendices
	26		Moved to Bonnerchi	
	29		Remained at "	
	30		" "	
	31		Entrained at Candas & arrived Contin & entrained to be sent (Contin Anne Cont)	

G Buts. Capt.
vy 27740/2.1
1/4/16

25th Divisional Artillery.

WAR DIARY

D.T.M.O.

25th DIVISION.

APRIL 1 9 1 8

Army Form C. 2118.

WAR DIARY
or
INTELLIGENCE SUMMARY.
(Erase heading not required.)

25th Div Divl Arty Trench Mortar Group   April 1916

Place	Date	Hour	Summary of Events and Information	Remarks and references to Appendices
Poperinghe area	1		Arrived Canteen Corner Camp at 1 A.M.	
	2		Inspections & drill	
	3		Met DTMO 2 Divst Division & went round seats	
	4		X & Y Btys relieved 3 Divst T.M. Bty + DTMO moved to Wieltje	
	5-9		In action registering & harassing fire. Very much shelled out of our	
	10		Attacked from west Fuel Farm - Hosp then side Hem and moved to Waterloo. Art + X + Y Bty moved to own camp M pers + 14 OR missing & wounded	
	11		Waterloo Camp	
	12		Moved to St Jans-Cappel DTMO attached to 23 DA HQ as Liaison Officer. HQ + 110 + 112 Btys Btys attached to 25 DA. Personnel supplied for Dirty dumps at Dranoutre - La Clytte - Poperinghe - Boeschepe - BERTHEN Camp	
	13		Moved to BERTHEN Sub Dr. withdrawn or Divry	
	14-23		Work on Swords at GODEWAERSVELDE & FLETRE	
	24		X & Y Btys relieved 1st Aust TM Bty in left Btn Sector (two gun in action) 2 Sect + 3e Sa (rested in Billet in FLETRE	
	25		Registry + harassing fire gun withdrawn for Right Btn Sector & placed with one other in front of METEREN	

Army Form C. 2118.

WAR DIARY
or
INTELLIGENCE SUMMARY.
(Erase heading not required.) 25 Sied. Bty. 7 Breed Brigade RSA

Instructions regarding War Diaries and Intelligence Summaries are contained in F. S. Regs., Part II and the Staff Manual respectively. Title pages will be prepared in manuscript.

Place	Date	Hour	Summary of Events and Information	Remarks and references to Appendices
METEREN	Sept. 26		Various targets in METEREN engaged with good result & nights bombardment	
	27		"	
	28		"	
	29		"	
	30		"	

J S Williamson Capt
a/D.S.M.O

30.4.16

www.ingramcontent.com/pod-product-compliance
Lightning Source LLC
Chambersburg PA
CBHW081501160426
43193CB00013B/2554